WHO ME, PRAY?

PRAYER 101:
PRAYING
ALOUD,
FOR
BEGINNERS

BY GARY A. BURLINGAME

WHO ME, PRAY?

PRAYER 101:
PRAYING ALOUD, FOR BEGINNERS

BY GARY A. BURLINGAME

Healthy Life Press

Who Me, Pray?, by Gary A. Burlingame

Published by Healthy Life Press
Website: www.healthylifepress.com
E-mail: healthylifepress@aol.com

Most Healthy Life Press products are available through quality bookstores everywhere, including major online book retailers. Copies of this book and a downloadable e-book version (or both versions packaged together at a discount) are available directly from the publisher. E-mail: healthylifepress@aol.com for information. To arrange quantity discounts or learn of other special offers, please visit our website: www.healthylifepress.com or e-mail us at: healthylifepress@aol.com.

Cover Concept & Inside Artwork - Gary & Corey Burlingame
Internal Design - Healthy Life Press

Burlingame, Gary A. (1958-). Who Me, Pray?

ISBN 978-1-939267-76-4

1. Christianity - Spiritual Life, 2. Prayer

Second edition, 2013. Printed in the United States of America.

for Christopher, who taught me how to pray

ENDORSEMENTS

If Jesus is our friend, then why don't we talk with Him more often? Perhaps it is because prayer as practiced by many Christians is a cold exercise rather than a warm conversation. *Who Me, Pray?* is a simple, down-to-earth guide that will help the ordinary Christian learn to talk with God in prayer. I recommend it.

– Eric Wallace, President
Institute for Uniting Church and Home

I think we all tend to make prayer more complicated than it was ever intended to be. *Who Me Pray?* is a simple and refreshing reminder that prayer is simply talking to God on a daily basis. In order to assist those who struggle with praying aloud (and who doesn't?), the author walks the reader through various aspects of the Lord's Prayer in simple but insightful ways.

Beautiful pictures accompany the discussion on prayer and the practical examples at the end are very helpful. This is an excellent resource for anyone who struggles to pray aloud, and a poignant reminder for all to not clutter prayer with religious talk but to simply talk with the God who loves us.

– David Trumbore, Ph.D., President
Effective Fitness Solutions, LLC - Bensalem, PA

Who Me, Pray? is an exercise in simplicity that Jesus would approve. Like His disciples, we all need to learn how to pray - simply, sincerely, respectfully, faithfully, and with hope. Gary Burlingame's little book will help many learn to communicate with God as if He were right here with us, which of course He is. Isn't that great?

– David B. Biebel, D.Min.
Author, editor, educator, publisher

INTRODUCTION

When a friend asked for guidance on praying aloud during meetings, I developed this short guide. It is for all Christians, new to the faith or well seasoned, who are uncomfortable with praying aloud. This guide is for young and old, and all cultures as it relies on what we share in common – God's Word.

With the world today in financial and diplomatic turmoil, with God being expelled from our schools and public places, prayer must become more and more evident and relevant in our lives as Christians.

The leaders of this troubled world must see us as a praying people; a people led by and reliant on their Lord God. We must be a people of faith, who come together in twos and threes, in homes and public places, and in churches, and in multitudes to acknowledge the one true God of all creation who reigns today and secures tomorrow for those who trust in Him.

– Gary A. Burlingame

WHAT IS PRAYER?

PRAYER, SIMPLY PUT, IS
EVERYDAY CONVERSATION
WITH GOD AS THE FATHER,
SON, AND HOLY SPIRIT.

IMAGINE BEING A TEENAGER
AND ASKING YOUR DAD TO BORROW
THE KEYS TO THE FAMILY CAR TO
GO SHOPPING AT THE MALL....

YOU ARE TALKING TO YOUR DAD

When you ask your dad to borrow the keys to the car for a few hours, you might show him your respect as you present to him your request:

❖ Acknowledge to your dad that you know *he's* the boss, that it is *his* car you hope to borrow from time to time, and that you are grateful that he takes responsibility for maintaining it.

❖ Thank him for letting you use his car in the past.

❖ Acknowledge your latest blunders, the ones he's likely to remember. Thank him for *not* holding those blunders against you, and for believing in you.

❖ Tell him that you value his guidance and wisdom.

❖ Give him your specific request; that you would like to borrow the car to go shopping at the mall for three hours today.

❖ Then let him rest until he is ready to give you an answer.

What do you think? If you approached your dad in this manner, do you think he would favor your request?

PRAYING IS SIMILAR TO ASKING YOUR DAD FOR KEYS TO THE CAR.

PRAYER SHOULD BE HONEST, CONVERSATIONAL, SPECIFIC,

AND ALWAYS RESPECTFUL.

PRAYER IS TO BE

PERSONAL AND CONTINUOUS,

WITH THE LINE OPEN 24/7.

WHY? BECAUSE GOD IS

EVERYWHERE AT ALL TIMES.

HE KNOWS YOU BETTER

THAN YOU KNOW YOURSELF.

SINCE YOU CANNOT HIDE

FROM GOD, DOESN'T IT

MAKE SENSE TO KEEP

THE COMMUNICATION

LINE OPEN?

NATURALLY AND CONTINUOUSLY

Some people get caught up in trying to impress others with how often they pray or how well they think they pray in public.

When Jesus was on earth in person, He criticized this attitude, and taught His followers to pray simply.

Too often we get caught up in rules, requirements, and expectations, which can hinder our freedom to communicate with God, and Him with us.

Sometimes we might even feel guilty that we don't pray enough when, in fact, we communicate with God more than we realize, as our spirit within is connected with His Spirit, continually. His Spirit even helps us pray when we don't know how to express our needs or concerns in words.

The bottom line is that God desires for you to pray naturally and unceasingly, whether in public or quietly and privately, sometimes without any words being spoken. The way to pray unceasingly is to keep your mind and heart open toward Him, since prayer is both speaking and listening.

DESPITE THE SIMPLICITY OF PRAYER, ONE THING THAT FRIGHTENS MANY BELIEVERS IS PRAYING IN PUBLIC, OUT LOUD, WHERE EVERYONE CAN HEAR.

Praying in Public

But preachers or elders or other church leaders are not the only ones who may pray in public. You can, too; and when you share your prayer concerns in a group setting, you are fulfilling one of the Apostle Paul's exhortations that when believers are together, they should pray. When this happens, it is a form of worship, as well as an opportunity to make known our concerns and needs, as well as to become aware of the needs of others we care about so we can pray for them even when we're not with them in person.

Public prayer, whether in a group of two people or twenty people, can be intimidating. Your voice might shake. You might be sweaty and nervous, fumbling with words and saying something that sounds awkward to you.

But remember, prayer is conversational. Prayer uses the same language and expressions that you use in everyday life. Prayer is to be a natural conversation, not a rehearsed recitation. This means that you can talk through prayer as you would in everyday respectful conversation.

The Lord Jesus Christ left us with a pattern or guide for prayer. You may know this guide for prayer as *The Lord's Prayer* or the *Our Father*. But did you know that He gave this guide to His followers because they saw how He prayed, and they, too, wanted to learn how to pray?

On the next pages, which you should compare side by side, you will find the Lord's Prayer in biblical language and a similar prayer in everyday language. When you compare the two, you'll see how prayer is a natural expression of our worship, spiritual desires, our needs, and our concerns.

Our Father

Which art in heaven,

Hallowed be thy name.

Thy kingdom come,

Thy will be done

In earth, as it is in heaven.

Give us this day our daily bread.

And forgive us our debts,

As we forgive our debtors.

And lead us not into temptation,

But deliver us from evil:

For thine is the kingdom,

And the power,

And the glory, forever.

Amen.

[Matthew 6:9-13, King James Version]

Dear Lord,

You are God and I am not;

You, not I, deserve all praise;

Your agenda, not mine, is perfect;

You, not I, control all things;

You rule everywhere, at all times.

Thanks for providing for all my needs,

For not holding anything against me,

And for helping me forgive others.

Please continue to guide and help me,

Keeping me from making wrong choices

Because *You* know what is best.

You are the Lord of my life,

Your power is always used for my good,

And I give *You* all the credit for the wonderful things

You do.

Amen.

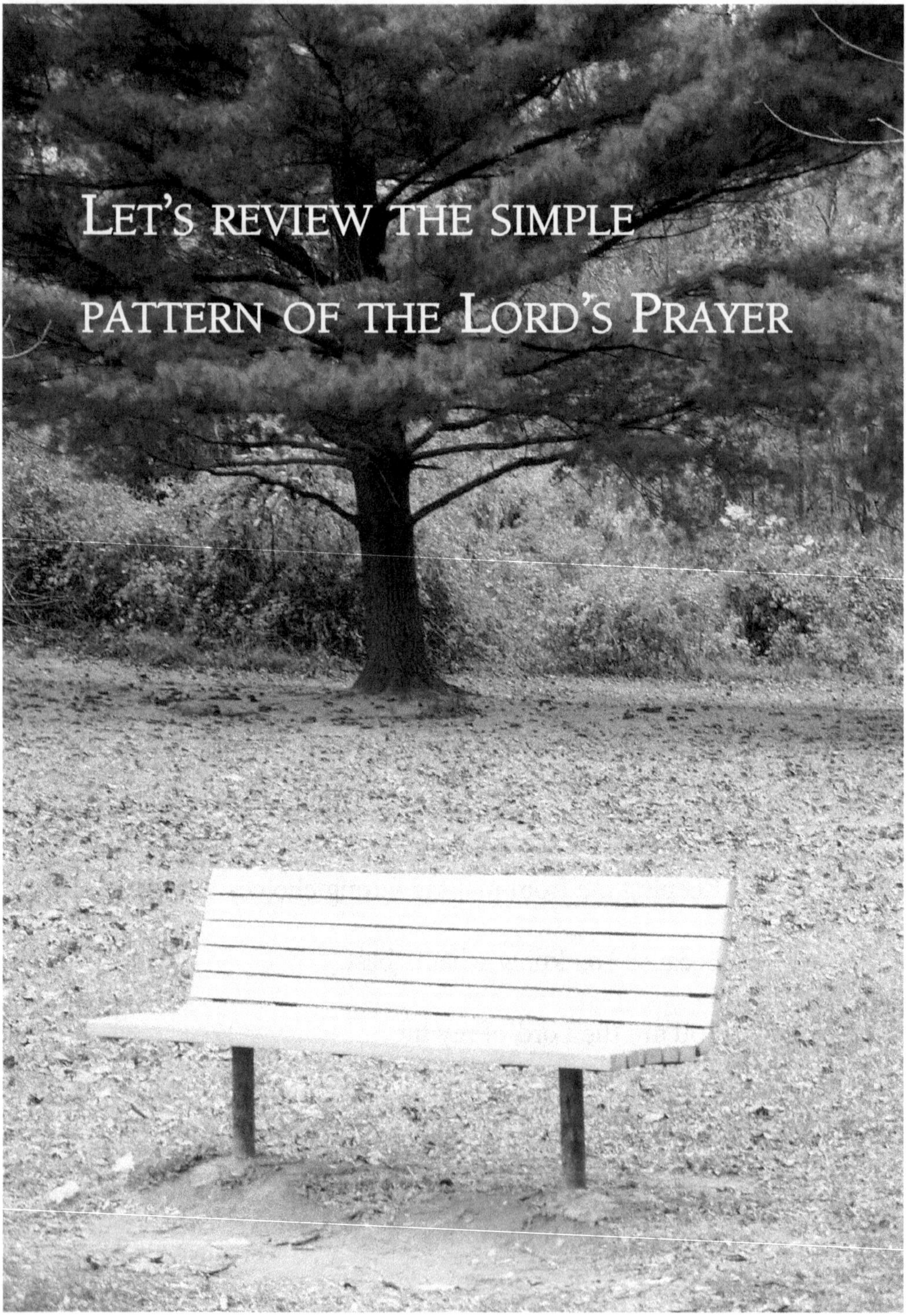
LET'S REVIEW THE SIMPLE
PATTERN OF THE LORD'S PRAYER

Acknowledge God as Lord of Your Life

Dear Lord,

Acknowledge God's Role in Your Life

◆ You are God, not me
◆ This is about *You*, not me
◆ Your will is perfect, not mine
◆ *You* are in control, not me
◆ *You* always know what's best and what to do

Thank Him for Everything

◆ Thanks for being faithful to me
◆ Thanks for not holding my sins against me

Ask for Help to be More like Christ

◆ Help me to show love to others
◆ Continue to give me guidance and wisdom
◆ Help me to avoid making wrong choices

Tell God He's Number 1 in Your Life

◆ *All authority is Yours*
◆ *All power is Yours*
◆ *All the Glory is Yours, as well*

End the Prayer

◆ Thank you and Amen!

EXAMPLE OF PRAYER FOR SPORTS COMPETITION

Dear Lord,

This is Your game, not ours;

Any success comes from You, not us,

For You are in control at all times.

We trust in Your guidance and Your protection today.

We acknowledge that the outcome is in Your hands.

Thank You for getting us here to compete.

Thank You for giving us healthy bodies.

Help us to demonstrate good sportsmanship.

Be our coach at all times;

Show us how to play hard and well.

For we play for Your glory.

And we play with Your power.

And if we should win, we dedicate the victory to You, in advance.

Let's play!

EXAMPLE OF PRAYER FOR A MEAL

Dear Lord,

You water the fields for the farmers' crops.

You control the seasons and the harvest.

So in a true sense, this meal comes from Your supermarket;

You even provided us with the money to shop.

All things on earth are under Your care.

Thank You for providing this meal for us.

Thank you for encouraging our family and friends.

Bless our gathering around this table,

And help us to have good conversation and fellowship,

Helping us grow in our love for one another.

This is Your world we live in.

This dinner comes by Your goodness to us.

We give all thanks to You.

Let's eat!

Example of Prayer to Start a Bible Study

Dear Lord,

We come together under Your leadership.

We come together as Your people.

We come together to study Your Word!

Your Word is the truth,

And Your Word is what we need today.

Thanks for the freedom to meet here together.

Thanks for giving us the Bible.

Help us to encourage one another to read it.

Help us to study it carefully;

Don't let our pride confuse our understanding.

Your Word is the greatest book ever written!

Your Word is to be praised

Every day and all the time.

Amen.

Example of Prayer while Helping a Friend

Dear Lord,

We're so glad You are our God!

We're so glad You're in control.

We're so glad You know what is really good for us.

My friend needs You more than he (or she) needs me

Because You know what's right for him (or her) to do.

Thank you for helping me when I needed it.

Thank you for letting me help my friend today.

Help us to be better friends to each other.

Help us, in turn, to help others

But keep us from following the wrong people.

You are the greatest example of love,

And You are our best friend

For all time.

Thank you!

PRACTICE TIME

Now that you have a guide for public prayer, it's time to
practice.

Imagine or recall a situation in which you were asked, or might be asked, to pray in a group setting or in front of people.

Practice praying aloud, using this pattern for prayer.

Just fill in the blanks of this guide using respectful language that you would use in everyday life.

Don't try to be fancy or impressive.

Just pray naturally, in a conversational voice.

Try using the guide a few times, and then try praying without the guide in front of you.

Acknowledge the Lordship of God

◆

Acknowledge His Place and Role in Your Life

◆
◆
◆
◆
◆

Thank Him for Everything

◆
◆

Ask for Help to be More Like Christ

◆
◆
◆

Tell God He's Number 1 in Your Life

◆
◆
◆

End the Prayer

◆

How did you do?

Did you keep it simple and personal?

Above all, remember that God enjoys the natural and honest prayers straight from your heart. Prayer should be a sincere and personal conversation, perhaps like two friends talking over cups of their favorite beverage.

Finally, those who benefit from hearing your prayers will greatly appreciate your simple, humble conversation with God.

BIBLE PASSAGES TO GUIDE YOUR PRAYERS

PSALM 23
MATTHEW 6:9-13
JOHN 17:1-5
MARK 14:32-36
MATTHEW 28:18-20
2 CORINTHIANS 1:3-5
EPHESIANS 1:16-19
EPHESIANS 3:14-21

PRAY UNCEASINGLY

When your mind time
Gets pulled away
By the pressures of the day
Don't get lost along the way
Just pray!

Pray unceasingly
It's common sense
Don't need to be
Quite so intense
Keep it natural
Exhale and pray
A word or three
Is all you need to say
When you pray

Pray as you drive
(Don't close your eyes)
Pray as you walk
(Don't stop to talk)
Pray in the shower
Pray for more power
Pray at your desk
(It's not a test)
Pray when in line
You've got the time
All through the day
In different ways
Just pray!

Eyes open
Eyes closed
In a crowd
Or all alone
Pray in the morning
Right out of bed
Pray in the church
Or in your head
Pray to the Lord
Read Him His Word

Pray and rejoice
Exercise your choice
Pray as you weep
(Shallow or deep)
And when you start
Right from the heart
Get to the end
Hit SAVE and SEND

There are many ways
For you to pray
So pray!

Pray with a child
Pray with a friend
Pray by the Spirit
Then say

AMEN

Resources from Healthy Life Press

We've Got Mail: The New Testament Letters in Modern English – As Relevant Today as Ever! by Rev. Warren C. Biebel, Jr. – A modern English paraphrase of the New Testament Letters, sure to inspire in readers a loving appreciation for God's Word. (Printed book: $9.95; PDF eBook: $6.95; together: $15.00; commercial eBook reader version: $9.99.)

Hearth & Home – Recipes for Life, by Karey Swan (7th Edition) – Far more than a cookbook, this classic is a life book, with recipes for life as well as for great food. Karey describes how to buy and prepare from scratch a wide variety of tantalizing dishes, while weaving into the book's fabric the wisdom of the ages plus the recipe that she and her husband used to raise their kids. A great gift for Christmas or for a new bride. (Perfect Bound Version (8 x 10, glossy cover): $17.95; PDF eBook version: $12.95; Together as set: $24.95; commercial eBook reader version: $9.99.)

Who Me, Pray? Prayer 101: Praying Aloud, for Beginners, by Gary A. Burlingame – *Who Me, Pray?* is a practical guide for prayer, based on Jesus' direction in "The Lord's Prayer," with examples provided for use in typical situations where you might be asked or expected to pray in public. (Printed book: $6.95 PDF eBook: $2.99; together: $7.95.)

The Big Black Book – What the Christmas Tree Saw, by Rev. Warren C. Biebel, Jr – An original Christmas story, from the perspective of the Christmas tree. This little book is especially suitable for parents to read to their children at Christmas time or all year-round. (Printed book: $7.95; PDF eBook: $4.95; Together: $10.95; commercial eBook reader version: $6.95.)

My Broken Heart Sings, the poetry of Gary Burlingame – In 1987, Gary and his wife Debbie lost their son Christopher John, at only six months of age, to a chronic lung disease. This life-changing experience gave them a special heart for helping others through similar loss and pain. (Printed book: $10.95; PDF eBook: $6.95; Together: $13.95; commercial eBook reader version: $9.99.)

After Normal: One Teen's Journey Following Her Brother's Death, by Diane Aggen – Based on a journal the author kept following her younger brother's death. It offers helpful insights and understanding for teens facing a similar loss or for those who might wish to understand and help teens facing a similar loss. (Printed book: $11.95; PDF eBook: $6.95; together: $15.00; commercial eBook reader version: $8.99.)

In the Unlikely Event of a Water Landing – Lessons Learned from Landing in the Hudson River, by Andrew Jamison, MD. The author was flying standby on US Airways Flight 1549 toward Charlotte on January 15, 2009, from New York City, where he had been interviewing for a residency position. Little did he know that the next stop would be the Hudson River. Riveting and inspirational, this book would be especially helpful for people in need of hope and encouragement. (Printed book: $8.95; PDF eBook: $6.95; Together: $12.95; commercial eBook reader version: $8.99.)

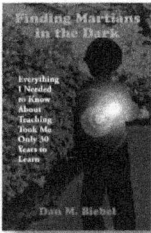

Finding Martians in the Dark – Everything I Needed to Know About Teaching Took Me Only 30 Years to Learn, by Dan M. Biebel – Packed with wise advice based on hard experience, and laced with humor, this book is a perfect teacher's gift year-round. Susan J. Wegmann, PhD, says, "Biebel's sardonic wit is mellowed by a genuine love for kids and teaching. . . . A Whitman-like sensibility flows through his stories of teaching, learning, and life." (Printed book: $10.95; PDF eBook: $6.95; Together: $15.00; commercial eBook reader version: $9.99.)

Because We're Family and *Because We're Friends*, by Gary A. Burlingame – Sometimes things related to faith can be hard to discuss with your family and friends. These booklets are designed to be given as gifts, to help you open the door to discussing spiritual matters with family members and friends who are open to such a conversation. (Printed book: $5.95 each; PDF eBook: $4.95 each; together: $9.95 per pair [printed & eBook of the same title]; commercial eBook reader version: $5.95.)

The Transforming Power of Story: How Telling Your Story Brings Hope to Others and Healing to Yourself, by Elaine Leong Eng, MD, and David B. Biebel, DMin – This book demonstrates, through multiple true life stories, how sharing one's story, especially in a group setting, can bring hope to listeners and healing to the one who shares. Individuals facing difficulties will find this book greatly encouraging. (Printed book: $14.99; PDF eBook: $9.99; together: $19.99; commercial eBook reader version: $9.99.)

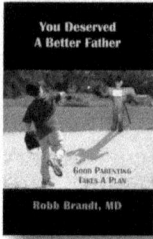

You Deserved a Better Father: Good Parenting Takes a Plan, by Robb Brandt, MD – About parenting by intention, and other lessons the author learned through the loss of his firstborn son. It is especially for parents who believe that bits and pieces of leftover time will be enough for their own children. (Printed book: $10.95 each; PDF eBook: $6.95; together: $12.95; commercial eBook reader version: $9.99.)

Jonathan, You Left Too Soon, by David B. Biebel, DMin – One pastor's journey through the loss of his son, into the darkness of depression, and back into the light of joy again, emerging with a renewed sense of mission. (Printed book: $6.00; PDF eBook: $5.99; together: $10.00.)

eBook Cover

Printed Cover

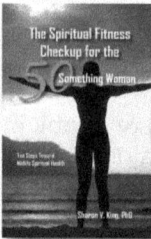

The Spiritual Fitness Checkup for the 50-Something Woman, by Sharon V. King, PhD – Following the stages of a routine medical exam, the author describes ten spiritual fitness "checkups" midlife women can conduct to assess their spiritual health and tone up their relationship with God. Each checkup consists of the author's personal reflections, a Scripture reference for meditation, and a "Spiritual Pulse Check," with exercises readers can use for personal application. (Printed book: $8.95; PDF eBook: $6.95; together: $12.95.)

Unless otherwise noted on the site itself, shipping is free for all products purchased through www.healthylifepress.com.

The Other Side of Life – Over 60? God Still Has a Plan for You, by Rev. Warren C. Biebel Jr. – Drawing on biblical examples and his 60-plus years of pastoral experience, Rev. Biebel helps older (and younger) adults understand God's view of aging and the rich life available to everyone who seeks a deeper relationship with God as they age. Rev. Biebel explains how to: Identify God's ongoing plan for your life; Rely on faith to manage the anxieties of aging; Form positive, supportive relationships; Cultivate patience; Cope with new technologies; Develop spiritual integrity; Understand the effects of dementia; Develop a Christ-centered perspective of aging. (Printed book: $10.95; PDF eBook: $6.95; together: $15.00; commercial eBook reader version: $9.99.)

My Faith, My Poetry by Gary A. Burlingame – This unique book of Christian poetry is actually two in one. The first collection of poems, *A Day in the Life*, explores a working parent's daily journey of faith. The reader is carried from morning to bedtime, from "In the Details," to "I Forgot to Pray," back to "Home Base," and finally to "Eternal Love Divine." The second collection of poems, *Come Running*, is wonder, joy, and faith wrapped up in words that encourage and inspire the mind and the heart. (Printed book: $10.95; PDF eBook: $6.95; together: $13.95; commercial eBook reader version: $9.99.)

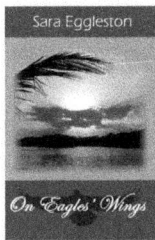

On Eagles' Wings, by Sara Eggleston – One woman's life journey from idyllic through chaotic to joy, carried all the way by the One who has promised to never leave us nor forsake us. Remarkable, poignant, moving, and inspiring, this autobiographical account will help many who are facing difficulties that seem too great to overcome or even bear at all. It is proof that Isaiah 40:31 is as true today as when it was penned, "But they that wait upon the LORD shall renew their strength; they shall mount up with wings as eagles; they shall run, and not be weary; and they shall walk, and not faint." (Printed book: $14.95; PDF eBook: $8.95; together: $22.95; commercial eBook reader version: $9.99.)

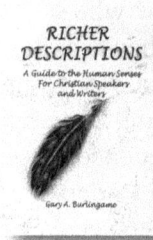

Richer Descriptions, by Gary A. Burlingame – A unique and handy manual, covering all <u>nine</u> human senses in seven chapters, for Christian speakers and writers. Exercises and a speaker's checklist equip speakers to engage their audiences in a richer experience. Writing examples and a writer's guide help writers bring more life to the characters and scenes of their stories. Bible references encourage a deeper appreciation of being created by God for a sensory existence. (Printed book: $15.95; PDF eBook: $8.95; together: $22.95; commercial eBook reader version: $9.99.)

Treasuring Grace, by Rob Plumley and Tracy Roberts – *This novel was inspired by a dream.* Liz Swanson's life isn't quite what she'd imagined, but she considers herself lucky. She has a good husband, beautiful children, and fulfillment outside of her home through volunteer work. On some days she doesn't even notice the dull ache in her heart. While she's preparing for their summer kickoff at Lake George, the ache disappears and her sudden happiness is mistaken for anticipation of their weekend. However, as the family heads north, there are clouds on the horizon that have nothing to do with the weather. Only Liz's daughter, who's found some of her mother's hidden journals, has any idea what's wrong. But by the end of the weekend, there will be no escaping the truth or its painful buried secrets. Printed: $12.95; PDF eBook: $7.95; together: $19.95; commercial eBook reader version: $9.99.

Life's A Symphony, by Mary Z. Smith – When Kate Spence Cooper receives the news that her husband, Jack, has been killed in the war, she and her young son Jeremy move back to Crawford Wood, Tennessee to be closer to family. Since Jack's death Kate feels that she's lost trust in everyone, including God. Will she ever find her way back to the only One whom she can always depend upon? And what about Kate's match making brother, Chance? The cheeky man has other ideas on how to bring happiness into his sister's life once more. (Printed book: $12.95; PDF eBook: $7.95; together: $19.95; commercial eBook reader version: $9.99.)

Your Mind at Its Best – 40 Ways To Keep Your Brain Sharp by David B. Biebel, DMin; James E. Dill, MD; and, Bobbie Dill, RN – Everyone wants their mind to function at high levels throughout life. In 40 easy-to-understand chapters, readers will discover a wide variety of tips and tricks to keep their minds sharp. Synthesizing science and self-help, *Your Mind at Its Best* makes fascinating neurological discoveries understandable and immediately applicable to readers of any age. (Printed book: $13.99.)

From Orphan to Physician – The Winding Path, by Chun-Wai Chan, MD – From the foreword: "In this book, Dr. Chan describes how his family escaped to Hong Kong, how they survived in utter poverty, and how he went from being an orphan to graduating from Harvard Medical School and becoming a cardiologist. The writing is fluent, easy to read and understand. The sequence of events is realistic, emotionally moving, spiritually touching, heart-warming, and thought provoking. The book illustrates . . . how one must have faith in order to walk through life's winding path." (Printed book: $14.95; PDF eBook: $8.95; together: $22.95; commercial eBook reader version: $9.99.)

12 Parables, by Wayne Faust – Timeless Christian stories about doubt, fear, change, grief, and more. Using tight, entertaining prose, professional musician and comedy performer Wayne Faust manages to deal with difficult concepts in a simple, straightforward way. These are stories you can read aloud over and over—to your spouse, your family, or in a group setting. Packed with emotion and just enough mystery to keep you wondering, while providing lots of points to ponder and discuss when you're through, these stories relate the gospel in the tradition of the greatest speaker of parables the world has ever known, who appears in them often. (Printed book: $14.95; PDF eBook: $8.95; together: $22.95; commercial eBook reader version: $9.99.)

The Answer is Always "Jesus," by Aram Haroutunian, who gave children's sermons for 15 years at a large church in Golden, Colorado—well over 500 in all. This book contains 74 of his most unforgettable presentations—due to the children's responses. Pastors, homeschoolers, parents who often lead family devotions, or other storytellers will find these stories, along with comments about props and how to prepare and present them, an invaluable asset in reconnecting with the simplest, most profound truths of Scripture, and then to envision how best to communicate these so even a child can understand them.(Printed book: $12.95; PDF eBook: $8.95; together: $19.95; commercial eBook reader version: $9.99.)

COMING FROM HEALTHY LIFE PRESS
CHECK WEBSITE FOR UPDATES

The Secret of Singing Springs, by Monte Swan. One Colorado family's treasure-hunting adventure along the trail of Jesse James (Late 2012).

I AM – Transformed in Him, by Diana Burg and Kim Tapfer, a meditative Bible study of the I AM statements of Christ (Spring 2013)

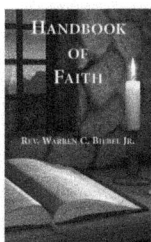

Handbook of Faith by Rev. Warren C. Biebel Jr. – The *New York Times World 2011 Almanac* claimed that there are 2 billion, 200 thousand Christians in the world, with "Christians" being defined as "followers of Christ." The original 12 followers of Christ changed the world; indeed, they changed the history of the world. So this author, a pastor with over 60 years' experience, poses and answers this logical question: "If there are so many 'Christians' on this planet, why are they so relatively ineffective in serving the One they claim to follow?" Answer: Because, unlike Him, they do not know and trust the Scriptures, implicitly. This little volume will help you do that. (Printed book: $8.95; PDF eBook: $6.95; together: $13.95; commercial eBook reader version: $8.95.)

Pieces of My Heart, by David L. Wood – Eighty-two lessons from normal everyday life. David's hope is that these stories will spark thoughts about God's constant involvement and intervention in our lives and stir a sense of how much He cares about every detail that is important to us. The piece missing represents his son, Daniel, who died in a fire shortly before his first birthday. (Printed book: $16.95; PDF eBook: $8.95; Set: $24.95; commercial eBook reader version: $9.99.)

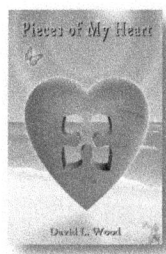

!!!!!UPDATE!!!!! Pieces of My Heart is also available in two volumes. Vol. 1 is the first 39 chapters of this inspiring book; Vol. 2 is chapters 40-82 of the larger volume. (Each of these new volumes are $10.95 for the printed book, $6.95 for the PDF eBook version; $14.95 for the set; commercial eBook reader version: $8.95.) Note: Couples have found it meaningful to read Volumes 1 and 2 simultaneously and then compare notes on what they have learned.

Unless otherwise noted on the site itself, shipping is free for all products purchased through www.healthylifepress.com.

Dream House by Justa Carpenter – Written by a New England builder of several hundred homes, the idea for this book came to him one day as he was driving that came to him one day as was driving from one job site to another. He pulled over and recorded it so he would remember it, and now you will remember it, too, if you believe, as he does, that ". . . He who has begun a good work in you will complete it until the day of Jesus Christ." (Printed book: $8.95; PDF eBook: $6.95; Set: $13.95; commercial eBook reader version: $8.95.)

A Simply Homemade Clean, by homesteader Lisa Barthuly – "Somewhere along the path, it seems we've lost our gumption, the desire to make things ourselves," says the author. "Gone are the days of 'do it yourself.' Really . . . why bother? There are a slew of retailers just waiting for us with anything and everything we could need; packaged up all pretty, with no thought or effort required. It is the manifestation of 'progress' . . . right?" I don't buy that!" Instead, Lisa describes how to make safe and effective cleansers for home, laundry, and body right in your own home. This saves money and avoids exposure to harmful chemicals often found in commercially produced cleansers. (Printed book: $10.95; PDF eBook: $6.95; Set: $14.95; commercial eBook reader version: $8.95.)

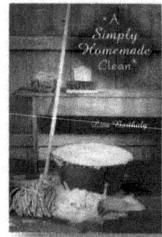

ABOUT HEALTHY LIFE PRESS

Healthy Life Press was founded with a primary goal of helping previously unpublished authors to get their works to market, and to reissue worthy, previously published works that were no longer available. Our mission is to help people toward optimal vitality by providing resources promoting physical, emotional, spiritual, and relational health as viewed from a Christian perspective. We see health as a verb, and achieving optimal health as a process—a crucial process for followers of Christ if we are to love the Lord with all our heart, soul, mind, AND strength, and our neighbors as ourselves—for as long as He leaves us here. We are a collaborative and cooperative small Christian publisher.

For information about publishing with us,
e-mail: healthylifepress@aol.com.

RECOMMENDED RESOURCES –
PRO-LIFE DVD SERIES

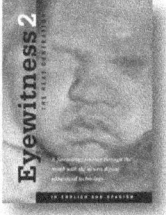

EYEWITNESS 2 (PUBLIC SCHOOL VERSION) – This DVD has been used in many public schools. It is a fascinating journey through 38 weeks of pregnancy, showing developing babies via cutting edge digital ultrasound technology. Separate chapters allow viewing distinct segments individually. (List Price: $34.95; Sale Price: $24.95.)

WINDOW TO THE WOMB (2 DVD DISC SET) Disc 1: Ian Donald (1910-1987) "A Prophetic Legacy;" Disc 2: "A Journey from Death To Life" (50 min) – Includes history of sonography and its increasing impact against abortion—more than 80% of expectant parents who "see" their developing baby choose for life. Perfect for counseling and education in Pregnancy Centers, Christian schools, homeschools, and churches. (List: $49.95; Sale: $34.95.)

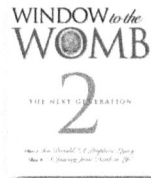

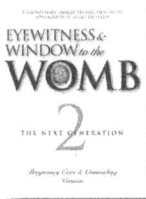

WINDOW TO THE WOMB (PREGNANCY CARE & COUNSELING VERSION) – Facts about fetal development, abortion complications, post-abortion syndrome, and healing. Separate chapters allow selection of specialized presentations to accommodate the needs and time constraints of their situations. (List: $34.95; Sale: $24.95.)

Unless otherwise noted on the site itself, shipping is free for all products purchased through www.healthylifepress.com.

If God Is So Good, Why Do I Hurt So Bad?, by David B. Biebel, DMin – In this best-selling classic (over 200,000 copies in print worldwide, in five languages) on the subject of loss and renewal, first published in 1989, the author comes alongside people in pain, and shows the way through and beyond it, to joy again. This book has proven helpful to those who are struggling and to those who wish to understand and help. Revised and re-released July 2010. (Printed book: $12.95; PDF eBook: $8.95; Set: $19.95.)

52 Ways to Feel Great Today, by David B. Biebel, DMin, James E. Dill, MD, and Bobbie Dill, RN – **Increase Your Vitality, Improve your Outlook.** Simple, fun, inexpensive things you can do to increase your vitality and improve your outlook. Why live an "ordinary" life when you could be experiencing the extraordinary? Don't settle for good enough when "great" is such a short stretch away. Make today great! (Printed book: $14.99.)

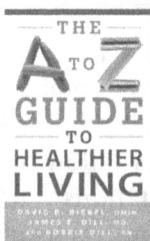

The A to Z Guide To Healthier Living, by David B. Biebel, DMin, James E. Dill, MD, and Bobbie Dill, RN – You'll find great info on: avoiding fad diets, being kind to your GI tract, building healthy bones, finding contentment, getting a good night's sleep, keeping your relationships strong, simplifying your life, staying creative, and much more. (Printed book: 12.99; commercial eBook reader versions: $8.99.)

New Light on Depression, a CBA Gold Medallion winner, by David B. Biebel, DMin, and Harold Koenig, MD – The most exhaustive Christian resource on a subject that is more common than we might wish. Hope for those with depression and help for those who love them. (Printed book: $15.00.)

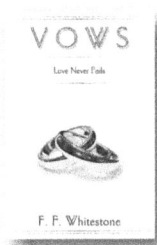

VOWS, a Romantic novel by F.F. Whitestone – When the police cruiser pulled up to the curb outside, Faith Framingham's heart skipped a beat, for she could see that Chuck, who should have been driving, was not in the vehicle. Chuck's partner, Sandy, stepped out slowly. Sandy's pursed lips and ashen face spoke volumes. Faith waited by the front door, her hands clasped tightly, to counter the fact that her mind was already reeling. "Love never fails." A compelling story. (Printed book: $12.99; full color PDF eBook: $9.99. Combination, only from publisher: $19.99. Other eReader options: BN.com and Amazon.com, $9.99.)

Our God Given Senses, by Gary A. Burlingame – Did you know humans have NINE senses? The Bible draws on these senses to reveal spiritual truth. We are to taste and see that the Lord is a good. We are to carry the fragrance of Christ. Our faith is produced upon hearing. Jesus asked Thomas to touch him. God created us for a sensory experience and that is what you will find in this book. (Printed book: $12.99; full color PDF eBook: $9.99; together: $19.99, direct from publisher; other eReader options: BN.com and Amazon.com. Available Spring 2013.)

God Loves You Circle, by Michelle Johnson – Daily inspiration for your deeper walk with Christ. This collection of short stories of Christian living will make you laugh, make you cry, but most of all make you contemplate–the meaning and value of walking with the Master moment-by-moment, day-by-day. (Printed book: $17.95; full color PDF eBook: $9.99; together $24.95, direct from publisher; commercial eBook reader versions: $9.99; full color, signed book: $29.99 [late 2012].)

Comments: *"My life has changed for the better and I am so excited. I am reading the word of God and tears fall out of my eyes because it's so amazing. I finally GET it!" –N.R. Orange Park, FL.*

"Your gift from God to share love and kindness will always be needed and I appreciate it." –Jo H., TX.

www.ingramcontent.com/pod-product-compliance
Lightning Source LLC
Chambersburg PA
CBHW060635030426
42337CB00018B/3368